D1085224

Maine
The Pine Tree State

Robin Koontz

PowerKiDS press™

New York

In fond memory of my summer in Skowhegan

Published in 2011 by The Rosen Publishing Group, Inc.
29 East 21st Street, New York, NY 10010

First Edition

Editor: Amelie von Zumbusch
Book Design: Greg Tucker
Layout Design: Ashley Burrell
Photo Researcher: Jessica Gerweck

Photo Credits: Cover, p. 22 (bird) Shutterstock.com; p. 5 Heather Perry/Getty Images; p. 7 © North Wind Picture Archives; p. 9 © www.iStockphoto.com/Andrea Pelletier; p. 11 © www.iStockphoto.com/ Philip Puleo; p. 13 John Kelly/Getty Images; p. 15 Mike Brinson/Getty Images; p. 17 © Jeff Greenberg/ age fotostock; p. 19 © MOIRENC Camille/age fotostock; p. 22 (tree) © www.iStockphoto.com/Nancy Nehring; p. 22 (animal) © www.iStockphoto.com/Paul Tessier; p. 22 (flower) © www.iStockphoto. com/Michael Zurawski; p. 22 (Dorthea Dix) Three Lions/Hulton Archive/Getty Images; p. 22 (L.L. Bean) George Strock/Time & Life Pictures/Getty Images; p. 22 (Stephen King) Larry French/Getty Images.

Library of Congress Cataloging-in-Publication Data
Koontz, Robin Michal.
  Maine : the Pine Tree State / Robin Koontz. — 1st ed.
      p. cm.
  ISBN 978-1-4488-0651-5 (library binding) — ISBN 978-1-4488-0734-5 (pbk.) —
ISBN 978-1-4488-0735-2 (6-pack)
  1. Maine—Juvenile literature. I. Title.
  F19.3.K66 2011
  974.1—dc22
                                                2009052048

Manufactured in the United States of America

CPSIA Compliance Information: Batch #WS10PK: For Further Information contact Rosen Publishing, New York, New York at 1-800-237-9932

Contents

A Rocky Wonderland

Which state is almost as big as all the other five New England states put together? The answer is Maine! People come to Maine to see its beautiful rocky coastline on the Atlantic Ocean. It has many bays, **inlets**, and islands. People visit the more than 60 **lighthouses** that dot the coast. Visitors also enjoy the state's thousands of lakes, ponds, rivers, and streams. They can boat, fish, swim, and hike in the wild lands of Maine. In the fall, people come to see the bright colors of the leaves.

Maine is in the northeastern United States. It is farther east than any other state. New Hampshire is to Maine's west. The Canadian provinces of New Brunswick and Quebec lie to the north.

Many people canoe on Maine's lakes, rivers, and streams. A canoe is a long, narrow boat. Canoes are quiet so they are good for fishing and watching nature.

A Hard Life

Many people have lived in what is now Maine. Hunters and fishers lived there over 5,000 years ago. Later, several groups of Indians, such as the Abenakis, Penobscots, and Passamaquoddies, lived there. They fished in the lakes, rivers, and ocean.

The first European settlements in Maine were started in the early 1600s. The weather was cold and life was hard. There were fights with the native people. Some of the first settlers died and others moved away. New settlers kept coming, though. Nearby Massachusetts owned most of Maine. Some people did not like being ruled by Massachusetts. In time, many people in Maine felt the same way. In 1820, **Congress** made Maine the twenty-third state.

Some of the first European settlers in Maine were fishermen. They caught, dried, and salted fish. Then, they sent the fish to Europe to be sold there.

Land of Forests

Maine's rocky coast, valleys, and mountains were formed thousands of years ago. A huge mass of ice, called a **glacier**, covered the land. It cut hundreds of valleys, bays, islands, and natural harbors before it melted away. Maine now has more than 5,000 rivers and streams. There are more than 2,500 ponds and lakes there. Moosehead Lake is the state's largest lake.

The Appalachian Mountains run across northern and western Maine. Mount Katahdin is part of this range. It is the state's highest mountain. Much of this part of Maine is covered in forests of white pine.

Maine is colder than most of the United States. It gets plenty of snow in the winter. There are not many hot summer days.

Mount Katahdin, seen here, is more than 5,250 feet (1,600 m) tall. The mountain is in Maine's Baxter State Park.

What Lives in Maine?

Trees such as white pine, fir, beech, and hemlock grow in Maine's forests. Lots of wildflowers grow in the forest fields. Flowers grow along streams and rivers, too.

The state's forests and beaches are home to many animals. These places have the food, water, and kinds of land that animals need. Black bears, coyotes, otters, and snowshoe hares live in Maine. There are more than 300 kinds of birds there, too.

The moose is the state animal of Maine. It is the largest kind of deer in the world. Moose can run 35 miles per hour (56 km/h). A moose has long legs that help it walk in lakes and ponds. However, moose can also swim!

Adult male moose, such as this one, are known as bulls. Bulls often weigh between 1,200 and 1,600 pounds (544–726 kg). They are generally larger than female moose.

A Busy Place

Forest **products** are a big part of Maine's **economy**. There are lumber camps across the state. Sawmills cut up wood for everything from lumber to matches. Maine is the top producer of toothpicks in the United States! Maine also has paper mills. There, people make paper from wood **pulp**. Factories make paper products such as cardboard boxes and paper bags.

People in Maine also farm. They grow crops such as potatoes and blueberries. They raise cows, chickens, hogs, sheep, and turkeys. People there also catch fish and shellfish, such as lobsters.

Tourists spend **millions** of dollars in Maine each year. These visitors shop in stores there. They stay in hotels, and eat in restaurants, too.

Lobsters live on the ocean floor. People who catch lobsters generally put traps on the sea's bottom. Then, the people come by boat to collect the lobsters they have caught.

Natural Food

Maine is sometimes called the lobster capital of the world. Many tourists come to Maine just to eat a lobster! More American lobsters are caught in Maine than in any other place in the United States. People use special traps to catch lobsters. Live lobsters are shipped from Maine to stores and restaurants around the country. Maine is also famous for its sardines. Millions of these tiny fish are packed into tins and sold around the world.

Blueberries grow wild in the fields of Maine. Native Americans ate the tiny berries. They ate them fresh or dried. In the 1840s, people started growing blueberries to sell. People now know that blueberries are good for your health. They taste good, too!

This girl is eating wild blueberries that she picked in Maine. Wild blueberries often grow in poor soil and in places where there have been fires.

Fun Cities

Augusta has been Maine's capital since 1827. The Kennebec River flows through the city. Old **Fort** Western is in Augusta. The fort was built in 1754. Today, it is the oldest standing wood fort in the United States. Augusta has many old houses that people can visit, too. Visitors also like the beautiful Kennebec River Rail Trail. People can hike or bike there in the summer. In the winter, they can ski the trail!

Portland is the biggest city in Maine. It sits on Casco Bay, between the mountains and the coast. There are lots of beaches and old villages nearby. Lighthouses shine in the night. During the day, people can do many fun things, such as fishing and boating.

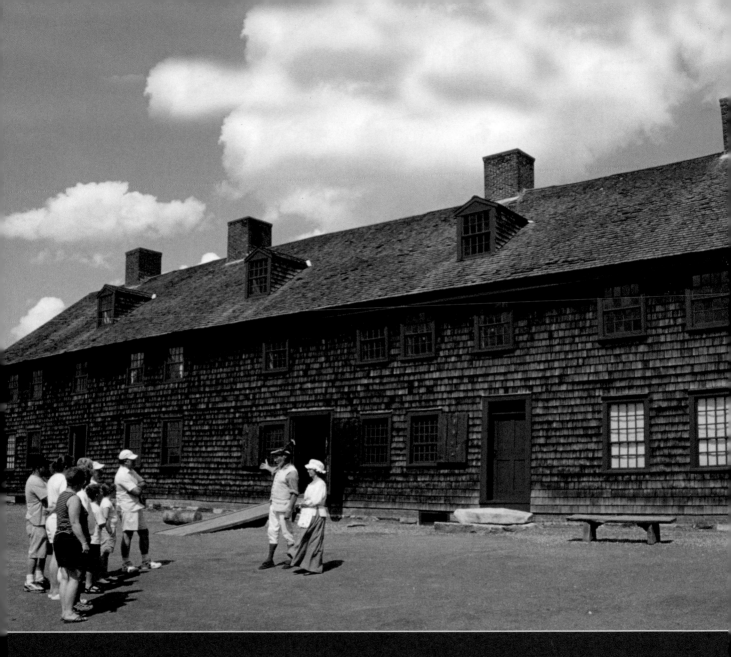

Visitors to Augusta's Old Fort Western can learn about the fort's history from guides. Some guides, such as these (right), wear the kind of clothing people wore in the past.

Island of Thunder

Maine's Acadia National Park draws many visitors. Most of the park is on Mount Desert Island. The park has 120 miles (193 km) of hiking trails. Visitors can climb to the top of Cadillac Mountain. It is the tallest mountain on the Atlantic coast of the United States. Since the Sun rises in the east, Cadillac Mountain often gets the first sunlight of the day in the United States!

Mount Desert Island's Otter Cliffs rise high above the ocean. Rock climbers like to work their way up the steep pink cliffs. They can see the ocean waves below. In a nearby inlet called Thunder Hole, the waves crash against the rocks. This makes water spray high in the air. Sometimes, it sounds like thunder.

In 1919, Acadia became the first national park in the eastern United States. At first, it was named Lafayette National Park. It got its present name 10 years later.

A Winter Wonderland

Maine is known for its snowy winters. People **snowshoe** and ride **snowmobiles**. They ski on snowy trails through the countryside. People can also race down mountains on snowboards. Later, they can sit by a cozy fire.

However, Maine is beautiful all year long. Wildflowers bloom in spring. Birds of all kinds sing in the trees. In summer, people can fish, swim, hike, and bicycle. They can watch whales and seabirds. Beach lovers build sandcastles. Everyone loves a Maine **lobster bake**! In fall, the state's trees blaze with bright colors. Tourists pick apples and drink fresh apple **cider**. They know they are lucky to be visiting beautiful Maine!

Glossary

cider (SY-der) Juice pressed from apples or other fruit.

Congress (KON-gres) The part of the U.S. government that makes laws.

economy (ih-KAH-nuh-mee) The way in which a government oversees its goods and services.

fort (FORT) A strong building or place that can be guarded against an enemy.

glacier (GLAY-shur) A large mass of ice that moves down across land.

inlets (IN-lets) Narrow waterways.

lighthouses (LYT-hows-ez) Towers with lights on top to guide ships.

lobster bake (LOB-ster BAYK) A party at which lobsters and other foods are cooked and served.

millions (MIL-yunz) Thousands of thousands.

products (PRAH-dukts) Things that are made.

pulp (PULP) Soft, wet, broken-down matter.

snowmobiles (SNOH-moh-beelz) Vehicles made to travel over the snow.

snowshoe (SNOH-shoo) To cross deep snow with light frames bound to your feet.

tourists (TUR-ists) People visiting a place where they do not live.

Maine State Symbols

State Tree
White Pine

State Animal
Moose

State Flag

State Bird
Chickadee

State Flower
White Pine Cone
and Tassel

State Seal

Famous People from Maine

Dorothea Dix
(1802–1887)
Born in Hampden, ME
Social Reformer

Leon Leonwood Bean
(1872–1967)
Born in Greenwood, ME
Founder of L.L. Bean
Company

Stephen King
(1947–)
Born in Portland, ME
Author

Maine State Map

Legend

○ Major City

✪ Capital

〜 River

St. John River

Appalachian Mountains

Chesuncook Lake

Moosehead Lake

Penobscot River

Flagstaff Lake

Kennebec River

○ Bangor

Mount Desert Island

Androscoggin River

✪ Augusta

○ Lewiston

Atlantic Ocean

Sebago Lake

○ Portland

Maine State Facts

Population: About 1,274,923

Area: 33,265 square miles (86,156 sq km)

Motto: "Dirigo" ("I lead")

Song: "State of Maine Song," words and music by Roger Vinton Snow

Index

Web Sites

Due to the changing nature of Internet links, PowerKids Press has developed an online list of Web sites related to the subject of this book. This site is updated regularly. Please use this link to access the list:
www.powerkidslinks.com/amst/me/